Contents

Shakespeare

The Tempest

Chapter One

 **A Magic Island**

A wild storm raged at sea. Winds whipped the waves into mountains. The thunder and lightning seemed to single out a sailing ship, to seize it and hurl it towards the rocks.

Sailors shouted to each other above the crashing fury of the tempest. Frightened passengers clung to splitting timbers. A king and prince knelt in prayer as the ship broke up. The sailors' desperate cries rose above the howling gale. "Mercy on us! Farewell my wife and children!"

Beyond the rocks and the sinking ship lay an island. A magical place full of strange music, with sandy coves and hidden caves, fresh springs and lush green grass.

Somebody had been watching from the island as the boat was dashed to pieces. Prospero, master magician, his white hair streaming in the wind, surveyed the scene from his kingdom.

His gentle daughter Miranda looked on in horror and then ran to her father. He was wearing his magician's cloak. "Father, what have you done?"

His words were reassuring. "Nobody has been harmed. Everything I have done is for your sake. It is time you knew the truth." He laid aside his glittering cloak and took her hand.

"Twelve years ago I was the Duke of Milan. You were a princess, heir to the kingdom."

"What foul play took it from us?" asked Miranda.

"My own brother Antonio stole our dukedom. How could a brother be so treacherous? I loved my books – they were dukedom enough for me – so I had asked Antonio to run the country. But he began to believe he was the duke by right. Like ivy choking a great tree, he slowly sucked all my power from me.

"He conspired with the King of Naples to get rid of me. And so it was that in the dead of darkness, soldiers abducted us, and set us adrift in an open boat. If it hadn't been for the kindness of one nobleman, Gonzalo, we would have perished. He had hidden clothes, food and water in the boat – and my precious books of magic. By some miracle, we landed on this island. And here we have lived together in our simple cell."

Miranda listened in amazement to this strange tale. Was it connected in some way to the storm she had just witnessed?

"Fate has sent my enemies to this shore. Now is the time for my revenge." Prospero took up his magic staff, put on his cloak and laid his hand on Miranda's forehead.

"Your eyes are feeling heavy … now you must sleep."

In a moment, she was unconscious.

Chapter Two

Strange Creatures

Prospero held his magic staff high.

"Come my servant!" he called softly. "Come Ariel! I am ready!"

And as if from nowhere, a spirit darted before him, a quicksilver spirit, as light as the wind.

"All hail, great master!"

"Have you done my bidding?" asked Prospero. "Have you brought my enemies ashore and scattered them around the island?"

"I have my lord. Not a hair has perished. And the King's son Ferdinand – I've left by himself, deep in grief, believing his father has drowned. Even the ship is safe."

"You have done well. There is more work."

"But you promised me my freedom!"

"Not yet. Have you forgotten what you owe me?"

Ariel's brightness dimmed as he remembered his life before Prospero saved him. He remembered the foul witch, Sycorax, who imprisoned him in a pine tree. He remembered Sycorax dying, and her son Caliban, half man, half beast, ruling the island.

Ariel cowered at the memory and begged forgiveness. He owed Prospero his life – and twelve years of service. The time was almost up.

Prospero smiled at him.

"In two days I will set you free."

"That's my noble master!" The spirit burned brightly again. "What shall I do? Say what, what shall I do?"

"Make yourself into a sea-nymph, invisible to all but me. Lead Ferdinand to our cave. Enchant him with your magic. Go!"

Like the whisper of a passing breeze, Ariel was gone.

Prospero turned to his sleeping daughter. "Awake dear heart! You have slept well. I must call Caliban to fetch our wood."

"I hate to look at him." Miranda shrunk back as the stinking creature of darkness slouched towards them, scowling and scratching his scaly skin with his long nails.

"This island's mine!" He bared his yellow teeth, muttering blistering curses yet cringing in fear of Prospero's anger. "You were kind to me at first," he whined. "And I loved you and showed you the secrets of my island. You stole my island from me!"

"You lying slave! You repaid my kindness by attacking my daughter! I taught you to speak but I could never teach you humanity."

"Yes, you taught me to speak, and I know how to curse!"

"Beast, fetch our wood, or you will suffer tonight." Prospero half raised his staff and Caliban flinched. He knew the agony of cramps that his master could send to torment him. He must obey. But dark thoughts of revenge swirled round his head.

Chapter Three

 **Love Strikes**

Ferdinand the King's son was wandering in a waking dream. He was bewitched by a strange and haunting melody, which seemed to have no source, but compelled him to follow it. The invisible Ariel was drawing him all unknowing towards his destiny – towards Prospero and Miranda.

"What can you see?" the magician asked his daughter.

Miranda had never seen another human being. She supposed that Ferdinand must be a spirit conjured up by her father.

"No," he told her. "It eats and sleeps and has the same senses as we do. This gallant was in the wreck."

Her eyes were held by Ferdinand's gaze. It was love at first sight. He knelt at her feet and offered to make her the Queen of Naples.

Secretly Prospero was delighted that his plan was working out so well. But things mustn't move too fast – their love must be tested. He pretended that he suspected Ferdinand of being a spy. "He's no king. He's a traitor," he said.

Ferdinand tried to explain. "My father, the King, is drowned. The strange music which brought me here spoke of his death. I am his heir."

Miranda couldn't understand her father's behaviour. "Such a beautiful man must have a good heart," she pleaded. But Prospero ignored her. "You will be my prisoner," he told Ferdinand. "I'll manacle your neck and feet together, and give you sea water to drink."

"Never!" Ferdinand drew his sword to defend himself. Prospero simply raised his staff – and the Prince was paralysed.

"Have pity!" begged Miranda, but Prospero refused to listen. "You know nothing of life. You have only Caliban to compare him with."

"My affections are then most humble," she answered. "I don't want anybody else."

Prospero raised his staff again. "Follow," he commanded. Ferdinand obeyed like an automaton, still gazing at Miranda.

"I will suffer anything if I can see your daughter each day through my prison bars. Her beauty is freedom enough."

**

On another part of the island, Alonso, the King of Naples, was grieving the loss of his son. As his friend Gonzalo tried to comfort him, they heard the hypnotic sound of soft music, which lulled them into a deep sleep. Strangely enough, it did not affect the other noblemen, Antonio, Prospero's brother, and Sebastian, the King's brother. These two treacherous men seized the moment to plot the murder of their king. They drew their swords, poised to strike.

Ariel's quick whisper in Gonzalo's ear foiled their plans. "Awake, awake!"

Chapter Four

 ## The Plot Thickens

There was thunder in the air. Another storm was brewing. Caliban shuffled along a lonely part of the shore, lugging driftwood and cursing his master. Seeing a strange figure approaching, he thought it was one of Prospero's spirits coming to torment him. He threw himself to the ground, hiding under his stinking cloak.

But the strange figure, dressed in cap and bells, was Trinculo, the King's jester, saved from the shipwreck.

Desperate to find shelter from the storm, he crawled under Caliban's cloak, despite its fishy smell. Caliban was frozen with terror. From their hiding place they heard the sound of drunken singing. Not Ariel's magic this time, but Stephano, the King's butler, washed ashore on a barrel of wine, and all the merrier for it. He saw a cloak with four legs sticking out. A monster!

By now, Caliban was shrieking in terror. "Do not torment me!"

"A monster that can speak English!" Stephano swigged from his bottle to steady his nerves. "I can take him home for a freak show! Come on, have a taste of this!" But where was the monster's mouth? Worse, it seemed to have two voices. A squeak spoke from its rear end: "I know that voice – it's

Stephano!" Out came Trinculo, and the two
hugged in their delight at finding each other alive.

Caliban was overwhelmed by Stephano. The
butler seemed like a god to him, with magic fire-
water. He vowed to serve him. Clutching onto each
other, the three staggered off to find the wine
barrel. Caliban told his new friends about
Prospero's cruelty. "Monster, I will kill this man,"
promised Stephano grandly, with a large belch. "I
will be King and Miranda my Queen. You two can be viceroys."

As they sang together in drunken celebration, a bodiless
voice joined in and then a haunting tune on a pipe and drum.
Caliban reassured them.

"The isle is full of noises, sounds and sweet airs that give
delight and hurt not." The music was irresistible. They stumbled
after it.

***

Prospero's plans were coming together. Through Ariel, he
knew all the schemes of his enemies and could see into their
evil hearts. His magic was drawing all the players towards a
final confrontation. Ferdinand and Miranda had proved their
love, and Prospero blessed them, but did not tell them that the
King was still alive. He was planning more tricks and teasing,
more weaving wizardry in a last burst of his magic powers.

Chapter Five

 **Forgiveness**

As the weary King rested with his followers amongst the trees, Antonio and Sebastian were waiting for their chance to kill him. "Let it be tonight," whispered Antonio. But at that moment they were transfixed by an amazing sight.

A wonderful banquet was spread before them by strange ghostly shapes, which invited them to eat. As they moved towards the table, there was a crack of thunder. A streak of lightning illuminated the fearsome figure of a gigantic bird with the face of a woman. It flapped its grotesque wings, and instantly the banquet vanished. Then the bird turned on the villains – Alonso, Antonio and Sebastian.

"You are three men of sin!" it shrieked. "Fate has belched you up on this beach to receive your punishment."

The men drew their swords in terror, but Ariel was too quick for them. They were unable to lift their weapons.

"You three supplanted Prospero. You exposed him and his innocent child to the sea. Now in your turn you are exposed to lingering misery, to grief worse than death, to everlasting heart-sorrow!"

They stared at each other in horror. Their great guilt began to work like a poison.

Stephano, Trinculo and Caliban were punished too. Ariel distracted them from their plan to murder Prospero by a bait of sumptuous clothes and jewels. As they pranced around in their finery, out of the trees rushed a ghostly pack of savage hounds, slavering for their blood. Prospero laughed scornfully at their screams of terror.

All his enemies were at his mercy, but he had had enough of revenge. "Bring them all here," he told Ariel. "And then you shall be free."

"I will return in two heartbeats," promised Ariel, as he whisked away.

Prospero put on the clothes he had worn when he was Duke of Milan, and faced Antonio. "I forgive you, though I can no longer call you brother. All I ask is to have my dukedom again." Alonso knelt to beg forgiveness. "I have been rightly punished when I lost my dear son Ferdinand."

"Ah," said Prospero with a mysterious smile, "I too have lost a daughter. But watch while I bring forth a wonder." Prospero pulled back the curtains in front of his cave. "As you have returned my dukedom, I will return a greater prize."

And there, sitting together playing a game of chess, were Miranda and Ferdinand. "What wonders!" gasped Miranda as she saw the handsome noblemen. "Oh brave new world, that has such people in it!"

And as you might expect in a tale of magic, everything ended happily. Alonso had his son again, and a new daughter-in-law. Even Caliban was forgiven. The only flicker of sadness was in Prospero's eyes as he broke his staff and threw his book into the waves. He had given up his magic. The tempest was over. Calm seas would take everyone home.

Break-time

 **Part One**

Mr Tanner was on duty that day. As usual, his voice boomed across the playground and his eyebrows waggled ferociously with every word he spoke. "It's springtime!" he roared. "So watch out for growing things, okay – shoots and leaves and suchlike. Treat 'em kindly, all right … and while you're at it, treat each other kindly as well. Remember, we've no room for bullies at this school!"

Nathan felt nervous just tapping him on the shoulder. "Excuse me, Mr Tanner," he said. "A couple of kids over there…"

"Kids?" Mr Tanner snorted. "What kids?"

"Over there," Nathan pointed.

"Those kids?"

Mr Tanner's mouth slowly dropped open. Soon, everyone else had turned to look too. They saw at once what the problem was. Three boys who were old enough to know better had climbed over the safety fence that surrounded the Nature Pond. Now, the two bigger ones were holding the smaller one upside-down. With their fists locked tightly round his ankles, they were lowering him inch by inch into the reeds that grew right by the water's edge.

Mr Tanner let out a hiss of breath. "Bullies?" he growled. "On my playground duty?"

"Mr Tanner…" Nathan tried again.

"Just shut it, okay? This is serious!"

He was already on his way. Trotting after him, Nathan didn't dare speak again. Neither did anyone else in the playground. The entire school stood dumbstruck as the teacher and his pint-sized pursuer hurried towards the Nature Pond. Not that the trio inside the fence even noticed. They were too absorbed in what they were doing. By now, the boy being dangled upside-down was almost at water level. If you listened hard enough, you could hear the splash of his fingers. His head and shoulders would be next…

Mr Tanner quickened his pace. This was a mistake. The grass round the pond was much more treacherous than the surface of the playground, especially after the weekend's heavy rain. Almost at once, Mr Tanner lost his balance. It wasn't a fall exactly – more like a striker being brought down in the other team's penalty area. But everyone could see the damage when he was back on his feet. Mr Tanner's heavy winter suit was smeared with mud all down one side, from the collar of his jacket to the turn-up of his trousers.

To be fair, Mr Tanner didn't say anything. Even his eyebrows were eerily still.

 **Part Two**

After his fall, Mr Tanner advanced more cautiously. At the top of the bank, where it shelved steeply towards the water, he dropped into a crouch. This called for a softly-softly approach, he'd decided.

"Okay, you little swine," he hissed. "Stop what you're doing at once!"

"Not yet, sir," one of the big boys grunted.

"What?"

"We're nearly there," said his helper.

"Now listen to me…"

"Got it!" squeaked the boy who was upside-down.

Quickly, making sure they didn't lose their grip, the other two lifted him upright again – or as upright as they could manage on a slope down to a pond.

"Is it all right, Mitch?" Nathan asked.

"It's fine, I think. A bit bedraggled, maybe. And scared out of its wits … but no real harm done."

"No real harm done?" snarled Mr Tanner.

"To the cat, sir," Mitch explained.

"What cat?"

"This cat," said Mitch, showing him. "Somehow it had got itself tangled up in the reeds. It was about to drown, we reckoned. We had to rescue it straightaway, sir."

"That's what I was trying to tell you," Nathan added.

Mr Tanner peered at the scrawny, sopping bundle in Mitch's arms. Actually, it wasn't quite a cat, nor even a kitten properly speaking – just something thin and leggy in between. Mitch was looking down at it as if he never intended to let it go.

Mr Tanner wasn't so keen. He did his best to keep hold of it

while he made his impromptu, open-air speech at the end of break-time. This was full of stuff about springtime, and growing things, and watching out for shoots and leaves and things like that. Also about how proud he was of Mitch, Nathan and the others. Apparently he'd spotted right from the start that something brave and special was going on. Everyone listened, stony-faced. When the cat was suddenly sick on his shoes, nobody laughed. It was never wise to laugh at Mr Tanner. Mind you, later that day, just about every kid in the school – one after the other – told him how sorry they were about his suit.

A Promise Kept

Part One

There was once an honest man; his name was Ifan. Times were hard and work was scarce, so Ifan had to leave his home and his wife and go off to seek his fortune.

Ifan travelled far and at last he came to a farm where he could labour. He worked long and hard until at last his master came to Ifan with his wage. It was one shiny gold coin.

"Here is your money," said the master, "but if you give it back to me I will give you a piece of advice that is worth more than gold."

"I'll have the advice," said Ifan, and here it is:

Never stray from the good old path.

Ifan set to work again. He worked and worked until his master came to him and he was offered the same deal. Again Ifan took the advice, and this is what it was:

Never lodge where an old man is married to a young wife.

The same thing happened once more, and this time the advice was:

Honesty is the best policy.

"Thank you," said Ifan. "I have worked hard and I have learned much, but now I want to go back to my good wife and sad I am to be going back empty-handed."

"Help me bring my hay in," said the farmer, "then my wife will bake a special cake for you to take home."

Ifan gathered in the hay and, true to his word, the farmer gave him an enormous fruit cake, saying, "Promise to take this home to your good woman. When you are at your most happy, break it and share it with her."

"That I will," promised Ifan, and he set off.

Part Two

He hadn't gone far when he met a rich merchant.

"Give me that cake," said he. "I will pay you handsomely."

"I cannot," sighed Ifan. "I have promised to take it to my wife." That's how honest poor Ifan was.

The two men walked on, and after a while they came to a place where there was a choice. The old road continued but now there was a new road running just below. Ifan remembered his master's advice and stayed on the old road, but the merchant went on the new one.

Now the merchant hadn't gone very far when a robber jumped out.

"Help!" cried the merchant.

Ifan heard him. "Help is coming!" he shouted. When the robber heard this, he turned tail and ran – much to the relief of the merchant.

"Bless you!" he said to Ifan. "As a reward, please lodge at my expense tonight."

But when they arrived at the next inn and Ifan saw the old, old innkeeper and his very young wife, he remembered his master's advice.

"I'll just stay in the barn next door," he said to the merchant.

In the dead of night, through a small hole in the barn wall, Ifan heard the innkeeper's wife talking. And what do you think?

She was talking to the robber! They were plotting the murder of her old husband.

"We can blame the murder on the merchant who is lodging here! He is a stranger – no one will speak up for him," said the robber.

Ifan poked his knife through the little hole in the wall and cut out a piece of the robber's cloak. Then he fell back asleep, not knowing whether he had heard all this or merely dreamt it.

But in the morning, all was clear. The innkeeper was dead and the merchant was carried away to the jail. Ifan went to the judge and told all he knew. Then he brought out the piece of cloth he had cut. It fitted the robber's cloak exactly. The grateful merchant was released and Ifan went on his way.

Soon, Ifan arrived at his own home. "Here you are at just the right time," said his dear wife, "for today I have found this fine gold chain in the woods. I think it belongs to the great lord yonder, and yet I would dearly love to keep it."

"Honesty is the best policy," said Ifan, and he and his wife took the gold chain and gave it back to its rightful owner.

Well, the great lord was so pleased that straightaway he gave Ifan the best job in the land. Ifan knew the time had now come to share the cake with his wife. He broke it and what do you know? Inside were the golden coins he had earned. So they really could live happily ever after.

Living Stone

Part One

"BOY!" The word swelled and bounced around the vast space of the cathedral.

"Where's that blundering boy?"

Ralph scrambled up from his corner behind a pillar. He hid the chisel and his piece of stone under a piece of sacking. "Here Master!"

The Master Mason had a bad temper and an ugly face. He caught hold of Ralph's ear and gave it a twist.

"You dob of ditchwater! Get up that ladder with more stone!"

The masons were working high up in the rafters now. The great cathedral was almost complete. Ralph loved it. A grey forest of stone pillars branched into the delicate tracery of the roof, so far away that it was hidden in shadows. How strange to think that the workmen who had laid the first stones were long dead. The blessed or the damned, they were all forgotten. Only their marks which signed each carving told the world who they were.

Ralph had always wanted to carve. Matthew, one of the masons working in the rafters, knew his dreams. Matthew had lent him a chisel and had seen his secret carving, fashioned in the likeness of their ugly Master. The head was like a misshapen potato, with warts encrusting the stubbly skin, and a lolling tongue sticking out like a shelf. Matthew had said it was good. Living stone, he had said.

Ralph hated his Master. But his father had struggled to pay the twenty shillings for him to be bound apprentice, and somehow he must see it out. It would be seven years before he had learned enough to work for a wage. Longer still before he could buy his own tools and have his own mark. That was what he dreamed of. A mark to tell the world who he was. Until then he must go wherever his Master went, do whatever his Master said, and keep his mouth shut. A nameless boy, a dob of ditchwater.

Part Two

"Get up that ladder!" The usual thunder-crack came Ralph's way.
"You gormless gobbet!"

Next to the ladder was the pulley rope. A block of carved
stone with the basket attached to it lay nearby, ready for lifting.
Ralph hooked the pulley rope onto the shackle. He could feel
the ladder flex as he took the weight of the stone. He climbed
upwards, steadying the pulley and keeping his eyes away from
the drop below him. He could see the wooden platform above
his head, and the solid legs of Matthew, working on the last
arch. Together they swung the stone onto the platform. It was
the keystone for the centre of the arch.

Matthew's rosy face was wrinkled with worry.

"Our measurements are awry. This keystone is made too
narrow." His broad hand spanned the gap, and then the stone.
"See, 'tis not large enough to close the arch." Then he smiled at
Ralph, a slow, secret smile.

"Say nothing to the Master," he warned, pointing down to
the bald head far below. It gleamed in the gloom like an egg.
Ralph wished he dare drop a stone and crack it.

"You must slide down the rope like an eel and fetch me
another stone. Fetch me your carving. Nobody will see it up
here. Fetch it fast before the Master sees what we are at."

And so it was that Ralph's carving found a place, so small and so high up that nobody would know it was there. Only Matthew and Ralph. And God, of course. When the cathedral was done, Ralph gazed up into the shadows, straining to see his secret. He hoped that maybe God might have a chuckle some day when He saw the Master's foolish face.

The Visit

Part One

Mum always said it was stupid to believe in flying saucers.

"Whoever would want to come here?" she used to say. "There's nothing to see, apart from cars, and a few elephants and penguins. There's no one interesting to talk to. And we haven't invented anything really new since Albert Einstein thought of lasers about a hundred years ago."

Typical Mum. No imagination. All kinds of aliens might have an interest in Earth. Old-fashioned interstellar explorers, for instance. Or galactic hydrogen miners, or the Stalking Warriors of Tiurf.

Mum wasn't going to stop me creeping out of bed long after bedtime and sitting at the window with the plastic binoculars I got for Christmas, staring at the sky for hours and hoping, praying, that just one of those planes landing across town, just one of those red and green twinklers low on the horizon was actually, really and truly, the personal sports-ship of Milky Way Adventurer and Comet Champion of the Outer Spiral Arms, Neerg Recorg. Fat chance. And why do aliens always have silly names, anyway?

One night I saw shooting stars. And I got good at the names of the craters on the Moon. But right through that winter and up until my eleventh birthday, I never saw anything in the sky I couldn't explain.

Then, in March, Granny came to stay because Mum was in hospital having the twins, and Dad couldn't boil an egg if you paid him. Our Gran was a tiny woman, with bright sharp eyes like a robin. She wore purple and gold slippers with toes that curled up like in the *Arabian Nights*. This, plus the fact she was small as a bird, meant she moved about the house without a sound.

So of course, on only her second night, she caught me. I had the window open in spite of the cold, resting my elbows on the windowsill to keep the binoculars steady. Her voice made me jump so hard I banged my head.

"What are you doing?"

She stood in the doorway, a dark silhouette against the hall's wan light. I hesitated. But it's wrong to lie to grandmothers.

"Looking for aliens," I confessed.

Her eyes glittered. She said nothing.

"I'll get back into bed," I said.

She glided across the room and closed the curtains. Then she kissed me with her dry beak of a mouth.

"You're looking in the wrong place," she said.

Part Two

I felt giddy all next day at school. If I was looking in the wrong place, that must mean there was a right place. If not in the sky, then where? Underwater? In caves? Inside volcanoes? I ran most of the way home.

"Gran...!" I began.

"Your tea's ready," she said.

"But Gran..."

"It can wait till you've washed up," she said.

"Yes, but GRANNY...!"

"Brush your teeth and get ready for bed."

I knew I was doomed. I knew she knew what I wanted to ask. I put on my pyjamas and made faces in the mirror. It was already night outside.

But then all of a sudden, she materialised at the bathroom door. In one hand she held my binoculars, in the other, my coat.

"Put this on. You'll need it." Her voice was a rustle of wings in high branches.

I couldn't speak as we went out of the flat and down to the street. My mouth fell open as she hopped over the wall of the park and led me across shaded grass to a patch of moonlit trees on the corner by the shops. And there, in the cover of the birches, she put a finger to her lips. She half-crouched among last year's leaves, pointing to a gap that gave a view across the street. I lifted my binoculars.

I couldn't believe my eyes. There, in the window of the greengrocer's, in that eerie blue light of shut-up shops, figures were moving – strange figures. I thought they were people at first. They were about our size. They had one head each.

But suddenly there came a flash and a ruby sparkle. And for a moment I saw clearly inside. Each of the figures in the shop had four arms. And at the ends of these arms were not fingers but things – weird, curving things. Yellow things.

"Granny," I hissed. "What are they doing? What brings them here to Earth?"

She looked at me solemnly.

"Bananas," she said. "They come a thousand light-years for the bananas."

Sci-fi/Fantasy

The Scribe

Chapter One

Click. The door closed behind them. And that was that. Neither of them could believe it. To be sent out of Mr Mooney's class for fighting was bad enough, but to be sent to the headmistress because of an argument over a stupid story!

Lee shook his head – in trouble for fighting with Hannah – how uncool can you get? She was the kind of girl who covered her school folder with stickers of horses and wrote made-up

names beside them in pink ink. "Misty" or "Goldilocks" or "Dream Dancer" probably. Not Lee's kind of names. Not Lee's kind of girl. He couldn't look at her as they headed down the stairs from 6B. She wouldn't look at him as they passed the school office and pushed through the double doors into the old part of the school, towards Mrs Reece's office. Her face looked red and angry. He hoped she wasn't going to cry.

Hannah felt a surge of pure rage. OK, so she had probably started it. But Lee was a little creep – the sort who pretended to be football-mad so his friends would like him – even though they were all pretending to like football too. The sort who thought only boys could have adventures, or shouted "yuck" when people kissed in films. She shouldn't have punched him. He probably thought it was cool to have fights. Gross. She didn't care if Mr Mooney sent her to see Mrs Reece, but to be sent with Lee Anderson…

Look at him! He was pretending she wasn't there as they walked down the stairs. Well, two could play at that game, Hannah thought to herself. His face looked a bit pale, though. Perhaps he was going to cry. And now here they were in the creepy corridor.

Why was this corridor so long, so dark and so empty? Did they build schools in the old days like this on purpose, just to make you feel small on your way to the Head's office?

"What's that noise?" Lee whispered.

Hannah smiled, "Just Barnstaple, the school cat."

She turned back to find him still rooted to the spot.

"Come on, Lee," said Hannah. "Stop messing about."

"There's something there," he said. "Look."

Standing in the shadows at the end of the corridor was an old man with white hair. There was nothing wrong with that … except that this man was transparent. They could see the door right through him. He seemed to have pointed ears, like a wolf. But he wasn't a wolf, obviously, because of the wings. Wings? And then they saw the eyes. They were deep red rubies, jewels of fear.

"Run!" said Hannah. She grabbed Lee's hand. They just had time to see that the old man was following, with a creepy gliding movement.

Crashing through the double swing doors, they saw the caretaker's cupboard to the left, full of hiding places. To the right was the school office. Mrs Frobisher would not take kindly to stories of gliding old men. But at least she was a grown-up.

Which way?

CHOICE 1 The caretaker's cupboard (Go to page 43.)

CHOICE 2 The school office (Go to page 44.)

CHOICE 1

The caretaker's cupboard

"In here," said Hannah. "Hide in here." Before Lee could argue, Hannah had yanked open the caretaker's cupboard and hustled him inside. The door slammed behind them and they were blind in the blackness.

"What was that?" Lee thought he could hear a voice outside the door. But before Hannah could reply, they both seemed to stumble forwards, as though falling down some steps. Lee threw out a hand, but there was nothing to grab onto. He was turning, head-over-heels, falling. But falling where? There was light from somewhere below. Or was it above? Lee had the strangest feeling they were falling upwards.

He could see Hannah nearby, a moth fluttering in darkness, twisting, trying to reach a flame. He saw specks of light in the night: hard, clear flecks of white and blue and emerald green. Suddenly his eyes made sense of it. These were not lights on a wall. He was not falling down a hole. Because what he could see were stars. The children were falling through space.

Below – or above – them, hanging in emptiness from the ceiling of the universe, was a pale and tiny sun, a ghostly lamp in the dimness. It was rushing closer. Lee couldn't decide if he was terrified or exhilarated. This was like flying. In fact, it was flying. They were not moths, but birds. If he tilted his arms like this … he felt himself swoop closer to Hannah.

CHOICE 2

The school office

"In here," said Lee. "Come on." Before Hannah could argue, Lee had pushed straight into the unbearable brightness of the school office. She opened her eyes expecting to see Mrs Frobisher's vexed expression. But the school office was not there. No desk, no computer, no "Late Note" tray, no Mrs Frobisher. Nothing. Just an aching bright light and a hum. It was as if they had

stepped right off the world and were floating in a cloud: a yellowish-gold cloud, like a summer morning dream.

"Are we dead?" Hannah wondered. She was more curious than afraid. She could see every detail of Lee's face, but it looked flat, like a drawing: there were no shadows here. Since they seemed to be floating, she tried to move herself with her hands. It worked. She drifted forwards, and when she looked back, Lee was following. Somehow the old man in the corridor had chased them into another world, another universe. Was this his home? She shivered.

The light was getting thinner as she swam. It was like rising up through a pool. And suddenly her head broke clear and she realised where they were.

Chapter Two

"What's going on?" Lee shouted.

"I think we … we must have fallen … through something."

"What sort of thing?"

"A trapdoor … in space," Hannah replied.

Impossibly, amazingly, they were afloat on the surface of a star. On all sides it curved away, a swirling mass of burning gas. There was a roaring in their ears, like the waves of a nuclear sea. And yet they barely felt the heat. Far above, they could see darkness: space and stars.

Right overhead were two moons, one dark green, one pale white. They were so low in the sky that the star's flames licked outwards to build a bridge of light across the gap, holding each moon like a ghastly balloon on a burning string.

"I think," said Lee, "I think that bridge might be the way out of here."

Hannah paused. Was this the same Lee she had teased in Mr Mooney's class? It was his fault that they hadn't finished that story they'd been told to write together. But now, he seemed like a different boy.

"Yes," she said, striking out for the fire-bridge. "Let's go."

Lee paused. Was this the same girl whose hair he'd pulled just now? They had been writing a story together. It was her fault they hadn't finished it.

"All right," he shouted back. "Which moon?"

They stopped their strange half-swimming, half-flying movements for a moment, and hovered in the warm swirls of gas.

CHOICE 1 The white moon (Go to page 47.)

CHOICE 2 The green moon (Go to page 49.)

CHOICE 1

The white moon

By the time they realised the moon was hollow, it was too late. Where the star-flames licked the side of the moon, a great hole was burned away. Into this the children fell.

Lee was expecting deep darkness inside; after all, the moon was mostly just plain old rock wasn't it? But he was wrong. The whole sphere was lit from end to end, with dazzling crystal and … Lee's mouth fell open.

"It's … it's inside out," he said. "It's alive. There's life here. Those are trees!"

Almost the whole of the inside of the moon was covered with a forest of drooping grey trees. Lee saw that on many of the branches, or flying in and out of them, there were small winged creatures. They couldn't be! But they were. The moon was home to hundreds of tiny dragons.

"They look sick," said Hannah suddenly.

It was true. The little dragons had mournful expressions. They barely looked up as the children drifted past. The leaves on their trees looked wet and old – grey dishcloths dripping from broken frames.

"Are the dragons waiting for something?" wondered Lee.

"They look bored," said Hannah. "Maybe they've run out of knights to fight, or maidens to eat."

Lee saw they were drifting to the ground. It was gloomy down here. The air was still and damp. The trees were bigger than he had thought, tall ghosts in the gloom. He looked up at them, and they looked back, frowning down at the children.

"What's that?" asked Hannah. Lee was getting used to surprises. In the side of a tree not far from them, there was a wooden door – an old-fashioned door, a door, in fact, rather like the door to Mrs Reece's study.

CHOICE 2

The green moon

By the time they realised the moon was hollow, it was too late. Where the star-flames licked the side of the moon, a great hole was burned away. Into this the children fell. There was a deep blue-green glow around them, shot through with gold, like a laser light show – what could it be? And then came a splash. The whole inside of the moon was filled with water, like an empty coconut shell filled with rain. Hannah realised those shimmering colours had simply been reflections from the surface of this alien sea, and now they were sinking to its depths.

At least breathing didn't seem to be a problem. In fact, it was all rather calm, Hannah thought. Here and there in the water, great flat fish like sting-rays flapped lazily through the falling light.

"They look sick," said Lee beside her. His voice made golden bubbles in the water. She looked and saw that Lee was right. The fish had a dingy appearance. Their scales were flaking off in places, and they swam slowly and aimlessly, as if they had long ago lost interest in the sea that was their home. They showed no interest in the children as they drifted by.

"I wonder how long they've been swimming here," said Lee. Hannah couldn't help thinking of the inside of the planet as a fishbowl. She saw now that they were about to settle on the bottom of the bowl. It had a sandy floor, from which, here and there, strands of coral rose to above the children's heads.

"What's that?" asked Lee.

Hannah was getting used to surprises. In the side of the coral closest to them, there was a wooden door – an old-fashioned door, a door, in fact, rather like the door to Mrs Reece's study.

Chapter Three

The children looked at each other. Surely this couldn't be the door to Mrs Reece's study? For a moment, they did nothing. Then Lee shrugged, turned the handle, and pushed it open. A room stared back at them – not the kind of room you'd expect to see on another planet. They stepped inside and breathed air, old-fashioned musty air, smelling of old paper.

The room was lined with bookshelves, and the bookshelves were lined with ancient books. In between, in the few spaces of wall that were left, hung portraits of schoolteachers in old-fashioned clothes. In the middle of the room stood a huge, proud oak desk. There was something familiar about it. In fact … Lee and Hannah turned to each other.

"It *is* Mrs Reece's study!" they exclaimed at the same time. At that second, the door swung shut behind them.

"Now what do we do?" Hannah asked.

"Well, if it is Mrs Reece's study, she must be here somewhere. Maybe we're going to meet an alien version of her next." Lee was starting to get excited.

"Hmmm, maybe," Hannah sounded sceptical. "Well, seeing as we went through such a lot to get here, we may as well

explore for a while. I've always wanted to look through the headteacher's desk!"

Lee was eyeing an ancient filing cabinet in the corner, labelled "Pupil Records". "First, I think we should do some research – this counts as a history project, if you ask me."

The children hesitated, finding themselves tempted by the prospect of exploring the desk and the filing cabinet. Both objects seemed to be calling out for inspection. But, which one first?

CHOICE 1 The desk (Go to page 53.)

CHOICE 2 The filing cabinet (Go to page 54.)

CHOICE 1

The desk

Hannah couldn't help feeling guilty as she slid her hand across the powdery surface of the desk. There was no doubt – she shouldn't be looking through someone else's desk. Dust gathered on her hands like the thinnest of woollen gloves. She looked around briefly. The computer was missing. So was Mrs Reece's embarrassing lava lamp. On the desk was a very old telephone, smiling at her with its circular number dial. A brass lamp with a green shade sat beside it. Its electric flex seemed to be made of woven brown cords. There was an empty inkwell, a rack of little coloured glass bottles, and to one side stood a typewriter, which looked as if it had been stolen from a museum.

Hannah sat down and gently held the little brass handle of the top drawer. She pulled.

Nothing happened. She tried again, this time gripping the smooth handle tight enough to chase the blood out of her fingers. After a judder or two, the drawer started to dislodge itself from its home. Hannah expected creaks and bumps as she slowly pulled the drawer towards her, but it moved freely, happy to be on the move.

The first thing her eyes settled on was a gorgeous leather-bound book, with lace-like silver lettering on its cover. She peered down, trying to make out the words, "The Sc...". What were the next letters? Before Hannah could find out, she was interrupted by a voice.

CHOICE 2

The filing cabinet

Yes, this was more like it, thought Lee. Whatever kind of adventure they were having, at least there was a chance to explore. All his worries about facing Mrs Reece, in a "telling off" mood, seemed to have disappeared, or at least to have taken the afternoon off.

He paused at the filing cabinet, a little put off by the sight of a keyhole next to the first drawer. Surely it wasn't locked? That just wouldn't be fair. The cabinet was only half his size, but its broad, squat body made it seem like a disapproving adult, watching him from an armchair and daring him to step nearer.

Eventually, he pulled at the top drawer, shaking a shower of dust into the air. Rather than jamming or squeaking, it almost rolled towards him, happy to be on the move. Lee couldn't help thinking that someone must have looked into that drawer recently. It was full of files, in alphabetical order, starting with "Abbot, Mary", and moving on through the "A"s to "Adams, Paul" and beyond. Lee was deciding which of these to open up, when his eyes landed on one file that was peeping out of the neat rows of paper and card. The little label was faded, but he thought he could make out the first few letters, "Ande…". Before he could get a better look, he was interrupted by a voice.

Chapter Four

"Well, well, well. Do make yourselves at home."

His eyes no longer glowed red. He didn't have wings or curious ears. He wasn't transparent any more, either. But it was still the old man from the corridor.

Lee dropped his hands to his sides, trying to look as innocent as he could. Hannah stood up quickly, like a soldier coming to attention. They glanced at each other, desperately. So, this wasn't Mrs Reece's study after all. They were, in fact, trespassing in someone else's space. And who could tell how that someone else would take it?

"I'm sorry if I frightened you before," the old man said. "I actually need your help."

His voice was rather soft and weak, and yes, it was kind. Lee started to relax a little; maybe they weren't in trouble.

"Who are you?" asked Hannah.

"I remember once they used to call me … Headmaster." He seemed to find it difficult to remember the word. "And later they called me the Scribe. But that was a long time ago. They're all dead now. It's my own fault."

Lee hesitated. "Who's dead?" he asked.

"The inhabitants," the old man said.

There was silence for a minute.

"Where are we?" asked Hannah.

"In school," he said. "Surely you can recognise it?"

"So this really is the Head's room," Lee said, brightening up.

Hannah continued, "But why all the old furniture?"

"And what about space, the planets…" began Lee.

The old man smiled. "A sort of shortcut," he said. "A shortcut through time."

"To when?" Hannah quizzed him.

"This is 1931," he said simply.

"Nineteen thirty-what?!" exclaimed Lee.

"1931…?" Hannah frowned. "This might sound like a stupid question, but…"

"No question is stupid, child. You may ask me what you will."

Chapter Five

"Are you a … a ghost?"

The old man smiled again. "No," he said. "I live here, in this year. I am the Scribe. Tell me," he went on, "do you write stories in your time?"

The children were embarrassed.

"We were trying to write one together in Mr Mooney's class," said Hannah.

"Only we … er … we disagreed about what to put in it," said Lee.

"Ah," said the Scribe. "Then this … Mooney … might have one."

"Have what?"

"A typewriter ribbon," said the old man. "Or a bottle of ink." He looked at them intently.

"Unless I keep writing stories," he said, "these worlds will die. Stories are the only thing that keep our many universes alive."

"Why stories?" Hannah asked.

"Stories write our past and our future. They describe people and things and when people read them, they keep all those people and things alive. Didn't you notice the animals on your journey? They're very sick, you know."

"Right," said Lee, starting to understand, "so this whole place can only exist if there are stories about it?"

"Yes, and I can't write without ink or a typewriter. And I can't fetch them myself."

"Why not?" both children asked at the same time.

"In your time, I am sort of … imaginary."

"Well, there aren't any typewriters in our school anymore," Hannah said, sadly, "unless there's one in the school office with Mrs Frobisher."

"Frobisher," murmured the old man. "Mooney…"

He spoke the words like magical charms.

Suddenly, he took a small blue glass bottle from the rack on his desk.

"Have you ever … been made very small?" he asked. Wondering, the children shook their heads. He held the bottle up to the brass light, and they could see a dark liquid inside. "Would you be willing to help?" the old man asked. The children nodded, wondering how they could possibly get him what he wanted.

He seemed to read their thoughts. "I can get us back there easily enough," he said. "And then it's up to you." He turned. He was pouring the liquid into a spoon. "This stuff works for five minutes. Mooney or Frobisher?" he said.

CHOICE 1 Mr Mooney (Go to page 60.)

CHOICE 2 Mrs Frobisher (Go to page 62.)

CHOICE 1

Mr Mooney

They stood on the floor below their class teacher's desk, but – fortunately for them – Mr Mooney was at the window, staring fiercely at some boys playing football outside.

"Quick," whispered Lee. "Onto the desk."

Hanging from the back of Mr Mooney's office chair was the hideous brown cardigan he so often wore. The strands of wool looked as large as ropes. "Not surprising," thought Lee. "We're only as tall as exercise books." A running jump took them into the cardigan and as quietly as possible they climbed to Mr Mooney's office chair, which began to revolve slowly as they reached it.

Feeling giddy, Lee and Hannah worked their way to the very edge of the chair and jumped for the desk. They almost didn't make it. Lee felt his fingers miss the edge of the desk, felt himself falling, and then laughed with relief as his hands caught the comforting handle of Mr Mooney's desk drawer, and he hauled himself up and onto the flat surface.

"Shhhh," said Hannah. "He'll hear us."

The desk was a maze of school books, and the children had to scramble over the register and make their way through an untidy heap of whiteboard markers. But they knew their teacher liked to write with a fountain pen. And yes! There at the corner of the desk, gleaming quietly, was a large bottle of blue-black ink.

"How are we going to get it down?" whispered Lee. They tried to lift it. It refused to move. It was laughing at them. "We'll never get this back to Mrs Reece's room," said Lee. Then an idea struck him.

Ink didn't just come in bottles. What about cartridges? If the old man only had a quill pen, he could cut the tops off the cartridges and get the ink out that way. It was the work of a moment to scramble back across the desk and ease open its drawer. There inside, besides a picture of Mr Mooney's grandmother, and a leather-bound book, was a little china pot full of ink cartridges. They found that by stuffing extra cartridges into their shirts, they could carry four each. They made the return jump to the chair and swung down the cardigan to the ground. Then they scuttled across the floor to the door.

Only just in time. Behind them they heard Mr Mooney turn from the window. They heard him make a noise like a startled parrot as he saw his desk. "What the…" he began. But they didn't wait. Tiny as they were, Lee and Hannah sprinted along the corridor and threw themselves off the top step of the stairs and down, like goats descending a mountain.

(Go to page 64.)

CHOICE 2

Mrs Frobisher

Hannah stared around her. A grove of gigantic table legs rose about them. There was some kind of threadbare carpet, which she didn't recognise. And then she spotted them: Mrs Frobisher's unpleasant floral sandals, with Mrs Frobisher's feet in them, tucked under the office desk. Each foot, Hannah realised, was as big as she was now. She could hear a deep rumbling sound. The photocopier? Did it sound like that to small animals? To mice?

Suddenly, she knew what the sound was. "Lee," she whispered urgently. "Don't look round." Being Lee, of course, he did look round. But as Barnstaple's enormous paw lashed out to trap him, he threw himself towards Hannah in a diving roll, and both of them ducked under the strut of Mrs Frobisher's chair.

"Naughty cat," said Mrs Frobisher, lovingly.

"What are we going to do?" whispered Hannah. "We need to get to the stationery cupboard. And we've only got five minutes." That was when Hannah decided she would never be rude to the school secretary again. For Mrs Frobisher's giant hand descended from above, scooped up Barnstaple, carried him to the door, and slung him out into the corridor. "Now!" said Hannah.

In a flash, the children were across the floor to the open cupboard. It was one of those metal office cupboards with movable shelves, and all up the sides were little round holes for the shelf supports. "Look at that," said Hannah. "Ready-made hand-holds."

She began to climb.

The first shelf was all envelopes. The second held boxes of paper, marked "From the Headmistress". But the third shelf was a scrap-yard: rusty spring-clips, strange rope-like bits of string, rubber bands like boa constrictors. This was promising!

Right at the back, beside an antique stapler, Hannah found what they were looking for: a great black metal reel. Wound round and round it was a band of material, red on the top half, and black on the bottom. It was a typewriter ribbon. They pushed and pulled at it, and eventually they stood it on its side and rolled it to the edge of the shelf. "Careful," said Lee. He was too late. With a clatter and a crash, the spool fell from the shelf and rolled out into the office.

There was a long metal locking rod on the inside of the cupboard door. Hannah didn't hesitate. She jumped for the rod, grabbed it, and slid down it like a fireman's pole.

Mrs Frobisher was frowning at the noise. But she wasn't looking down as the two children raced out across the floor and pushed the typewriter ribbon, like a hoop, through the door of the office and along the main school corridor.

(Go to page 64.)

Chapter Five *continued*

Then there was just the corridor to negotiate. Just? Children were milling about, and it was a tough job dodging all the trainers. "Doesn't anyone ever look down?" wondered Hannah. But no one trod on them. And there was no sign of Barnstaple.

They had just got to Mrs Reece's door when they realised the five minutes were up and that both had returned to their usual sizes. Lee and Hannah shared a smile – a smile of relief and satisfaction at finding what the old man needed, and doing it without being caught.

At that moment, the study door opened and the old man leaned out and swiftly relieved them of their find. "Always finish your stories," he said, and slammed the door again.

"Wait!" began Lee. "What about…"

"Wait!" said Hannah as the door closed again. Impatiently, they rapped their fists on it. Nothing happened at first. Then the door was flung open and they glimpsed Mrs Reece's study as it had always been.

"What on Earth do you mean knocking like that?!" boomed the headmistress.

"Well…" began Lee and Hannah, in unison.